TABLE OF CO

1. 1-Page Summary of The 5 AM

2. Full Summary of The 5 AM Cl

- Big Idea #1: A chance meeting drew a disillusioned entrepreneur and a frustrated artist to the secrets of the 5 AM club.
- Big Idea #2: The solitude and enhanced brain state that you'll experience at 5:00 a.m. will help you perform like the elite.
- Big Idea #3: Historymakers capitalize on their talents, avoid distraction, achieve every day and master themselves.
- Big Idea #4: Giving attention to each of the four interior empires will allow you to master yourself and your chosen field.
- Big Idea #5: The 20/20/20 formula ensures that waking up at 5:00 a.m. generates incredible results.
- Big Idea #6: Embracing sleep and the "twin-cycle of elite performance" is essential to maximizing the potential of the 5 AM club.

3. Three biggest lessons learned from this book

- Waking up at 5 a.m. will provide you with the solitude and improved brain state to perform like the pros.
- Balance your four "interior empires" to achieve self-mastery.
- Don't waste time when you wake up early, use the 20/20/20 formula.

4. Is the 5 a.m. Club Right For You?

5. Is the 5am Club Worth Getting out of Bed For?
6. Benefits of Waking Up at 5am
7. Some foods that help in sleeping
8. Book Review: The 5AM Club

1-Page Summary of The 5 AM Club

Overview

The 5 AM Club is a story about success, not just financial or professional success but true success. People who are successful become heroes and everyone can be one if they embrace discomfort by focusing their energy on self improvement. The first habit to improve yourself is waking up at 5 AM so you have time to exercise, meditate and read before starting your day.

As you read this, keep in mind the insights of the 5 AM Club. They focus on four things: improving upon your natural talents, freeing yourself from distractions, mastering your craft and building each day's successes on yesterday's progress. To create new habits, choose a trigger (something that will remind you to do something), a ritual (the actual thing that you'll do) and a reward (a positive reinforcement for doing it). Then turn these habits into triggers for further habits by making them part of your life. The 20/20/20 formula is made up of three parts: first exercise intensely for 20 minutes; then spend 20 minutes reflecting on what has been achieved so far; lastly, study or learn something related to the goal for 20 minutes. This method should be practiced every day at least once during the week. Another way to boost productivity is through using the 90/90/1 rule which requires spending 90 minutes practicing one skill per day while only using 10% of our time thinking about other things like email or social media. Use 60 minute cycles where you work with intense concentration followed by short breaks as needed during those periods when working becomes difficult due to fatigue or boredom. Finally, use traffic university as an opportunity to learn instead of letting yourself become distracted by all kinds of information available online.

A Daily Philosophy on Becoming Legendary

In the 5 AM Club parable, an Artist and Entrepreneur attend a seminar hosted by the Spellbinder. The Spellbinder lectures on how mindset is important: Regardless of your past, you can adopt a fearless mentality that will help you take action to achieve success. You must be willing to be uncomfortable in order to overcome fear. In fact, opportunities will arise when you are most uncomfortable.

At the end of his speech, the Spellbinder collapsed. Afterward, the Artist and Entrepreneur met a strange homeless man outside who seemed to know everything about what he had to teach. He told them that they should spend more time with people who understand them and do things that make them happy. If you surround yourself with good influences, you'll be happier and more productive in your work.

Karen had a dream of becoming a nurse. However, she was surrounded by people who didn't value education and were more interested in partying. She eventually decided to go back to school and become a nurse. In order to do this, she needed to make some changes that would be uncomfortable for her, but it was worth it because the skills she learned at nursing school improved her life significantly.

The artist and the entrepreneur had a conversation with a homeless man after they saw his performance. The next day, they were picked up in a limo to fly on a private jet to Mauritius. They were given five rules by the man: Distraction kills creativity; excuses will never produce genius; change is hard at first but beautiful when it's done; if you want to rise above others, you must challenge yourself more than they challenge themselves;

and the point where you feel like giving up is exactly the point at which you should proceed toward your goals.

The 5 AM Method: The Morning Routine of World Builders

A homeless man named Stone Riley was actually a very rich and influential man who had one of the best mentors in the world. The homeless man's first lesson for his mentor was to wake up early every day.

The early morning hours are a great time to get an advantage over others. Most people sleep during that time, so you can strategize and work on your goals without the distractions of daily life. It's also a good way to build better habits, which will help you achieve success in other areas of your life.

That evening, the Artist and Entrepreneur bonded. The Entrepreneur was afraid of being abandoned by her father. She also had a board threatening to remove her from power in the company that she founded and nurtured to astronomical success. For his part, the Artist lost his sense of creativity when he was young, but since then developed resentment towards authority figures instead of regaining his creative side. This fear limited Riley's new students with their dreams

Course:

The next day, Riley taught the Artist and the Entrepreneur how to pay attention to the details of their work. If you notice more things about a situation, then you have more information to make better decisions with. Better decisions lead to better results.

Monique was an expert at her bakery. She knew what the customers wanted, but she didn't track sales. One day, she decided to look into the point-of-sale system and discovered patterns in customer purchases. By paying attention to details, Monique could create a production schedule that increased sales by 20%.

Next, the speaker explained how to be a history maker. The first step is to capitalize on your natural talents and grow them into something greater than what they are naturally. You should work hard at improving upon your gifts so that you can become an exceptional person. Next, you have to free yourself from distractions in order to focus more clearly on what's important for achieving success. Every day, practice skills that will help you achieve personal mastery and prepare yourself physically and mentally for the things that matter most when it comes time to do them. Finally, make sure each day builds on the last by practicing consistency as well as small improvements every single day without fail.

The 5 AM Club Discovers the Habit Installation Protocol

Riley took the author to see the Taj Mahal in Agra and explained how habits are formed. Habits come from consistency and willpower. If you have little willpower, it's OK; all that matters is that you keep building your willpower by exercising it over time. The Taj Mahal serves as a useful metaphor for habit-building: It took Shah Jahan two decades to complete the mausoleum, but he stayed consistent because he wanted to express his love for his late wife. You can't just build habits; you must care deeply about them and follow through with your plans.

Habits have four steps. First, a person must decide on an action that will trigger the habit (the second step). After doing this action, the third step is to reward oneself for doing it. The fourth and final step is to repeat it. This process can be used to turn habits into triggers for more habits, which builds success upon success.

The 5 AM Club Learns the 20/20/20 Formula

Riley took the artist and entrepreneur, who were in love, to Rome. He had fallen in love with his wife here before she died. In this city they met a man named 20/20/20 – after waking up at 5 AM you spend 20 minutes on exercise, 20 minutes on reflection and then another 20 minutes on self-improvement (reading or listening to podcasts).

The 5 AM Club is Mentored on the Tactics of Life-long Genius

A couple from São Paulo, Brazil were able to make changes in their lives. They woke up early and focused on the important things that they needed to get done every day. By practicing a few habits, they became more productive than ever before. The Artist and Entrepreneur also used some of Riley's tricks while he was coaching them. For example, the 90/90/1 rule helped them become better at what they do by dedicating time each day to practice it for 90 days straight. Also, 60 minutes of intense focus followed by 10 minutes of rest is another one of Riley's tricks; this helps people stay focused throughout the whole day instead of becoming fatigued after a long period without rest or recovery time. It's not just about working hard but knowing when you need to take breaks as well so you can come back stronger than you were before taking those breaks. Traffic University is another trick that helps people learn something new during their commute home from work or school each night because most people don't use this downtime productively. Finally, there are certain systems that help keep track of your week like scheduling out 30 minutes every Sunday for creating your schedule which gives priority to tasks based on how important they are compared with other tasks in your life.

Conclusion

Success for the sake of success isn't enough. Instead, you should be striving to change the world by becoming a hero. To do that, you need to work hard and become really good at something that matters. It's important to remember that history makers are masters of their craft who focus on improving themselves every day so they can be better than yesterday. Setting up new habits is easy: just choose your trigger (what will make it happen), ritual (how you'll accomplish it), and reward (why it's worth doing). Then turn those into triggers for even more habits! The most productive people get up early and spend 20 minutes exercising, reflecting on what they've learned in the past year, and studying one thing before moving onto other tasks during the rest of their morning routine. Afternoons are spent working intensely with breaks every 90 minutes for 10-minute periods of deep rest or reflection. Finally, evenings are used as an opportunity to learn something new while commuting between home and work or school because traffic gives us time we don't often have otherwise!

You know how some people seem like they're always busy? That's because they take advantage of these techniques by using them each week in order to build a beautiful week full of productivity without having to waste time trying things out over several months or years.

Full Summary of The 5 AM Club

Overview

There was once a billionaire who reached the top of his field. He achieved success in both his professional and personal life. He would leave a legacy for the world, but he attributed it to an unusual morning routine that started at 5:00 AM and included exercise and mental focus.

The author explains how to join the 5 AM club. He/she suggests that you learn how to rise early each day and use your time wisely. The author emphasizes that you can be like elite performers who get ahead by making the most of their morning hours, which are typically used for sleeping or wasting time with social media.

Here are four important points that will help you to be more productive. First, being distracted reduces your productivity. Second, slowing down your brain helps with focus and concentration. Third, establishing a routine is important for success. Finally, it's critical to eliminate distractions in order to become successful.

Big Idea #1: A chance meeting drew a disillusioned entrepreneur and a frustrated artist to the secrets of the 5 AM club.

This is a story about three people. One of them, the Spellbinder, is a successful businessman who has helped many others to succeed in business. The other two are an artist and an entrepreneur. They meet at the conference where the Spellbinder gives his speech on how to live an extraordinary life. The artist and the entrepreneur don't know that they're talking with a billionaire disguised as a poor man because he wants to remind himself that money isn't everything. He wears cheap clothes and carries only one thing that's expensive—a watch worth thousands of dollars.

The billionaire tells them something interesting: Successful people make things happen for themselves instead of waiting for good things to happen by chance or hoping that someone else will help them achieve their dreams.

A billionaire and an artist were curious about a guru who was giving advice to their mentor. They went to him and asked what he had learned from the guru that he didn't know before. The billionaire, in turn, told them about how his mentor taught him one thing that changed everything for him: having a solid morning routine is the most important thing you can do for yourself personally or professionally. He then offered to teach them more if they came with him on vacation so they could learn it themselves firsthand at 5 am..

The entrepreneur and the artist were a little skeptical about flying in a private jet, but they were soon convinced when they arrived at an airport to find a Rolls-Royce waiting for them. The chauffeur drove them to their plane, which had the logo "5AC."

An entrepreneur asked his chauffeur what the logo meant on the side of their car, and he explained it stood for "The 5 AM Club." They began talking about how a morning routine can change one's life.

Big Idea #2: The solitude and enhanced brain state that you'll experience at 5:00 a.m. will help you perform like the elite.

Early in the morning, a billionaire told an artist and entrepreneur how he had learned to achieve greatness by getting up at 5:00. He said that this habit promoted his creativity, doubled his energy, and tripled his productivity.

A billionaire once told a group of people that many great writers and musicians, including John Grisham and Wolfgang Amadeus Mozart, have understood the value of getting up early. They've found that their minds are sharper in the morning than later on in the day. Because we're so busy throughout the day, our brains get distracted by all sorts of things—work, news, social media—and before you know it, we can't really focus on anything anymore. But if you wake up early enough to do one thing without distraction for an hour or two while your mind is fresh (since you haven't been bombarded with distractions yet), then you can accomplish more than usual during your day.

Transient hypofrontality is a state of mind that allows you to focus better at 5:00 in the morning.

If you get up early in the morning, your brain will be stimulated by the peace of daybreak. This causes a change in neurotransmitters and allows for flow to happen. Flow is an elite mind-set that top performers live in when they are at their best. If you can harness this state, then getting up early will help you be more productive and focused throughout your entire day.

If you want to be successful, you should get up early. Most people aren't willing to do that so this gives you a competitive advantage over them. Now let's look at how we can achieve greatness and become true historymakers by doing what only 5% of entrepreneurs, artists and others are willing to do.

Big Idea #3: Historymakers capitalize on their talents, avoid distraction, achieve every day and master themselves.

On a beautiful day in Mauritius, the entrepreneur, artist and billionaire gathered to talk about how they became successful. The billionaire said that it's not just talent or giftedness that makes someone great; self-discipline and perseverance are also important. He explained that people need to capitalize on their gifts rather than thinking they don't have what it takes. Additionally, being free from distractions is key because too many people waste time on technology and social media when they should be focusing on their work projects. They become purists who concentrate on one amazing project at a time instead of doing many good ones. In order to do this effectively, he suggests turning off your notifications and canceling pointless meetings so you can focus more intently on what's most important in life—your family, friends and career goals for example. If you want to win big, you must focus relentlessly on these things every single day by joining the 5 am club (early morning group of hard workers)

Thirdly, the truly great understand how important it is to do things every day. They don't wait for a big event or special occasion to make progress on their goals. Instead, they focus on making small improvements daily and over time these add up to significant gains.

The billionaire also talked about the importance of personal mastery. In order to master a skill, one must practice it for at least 2.75 hours every day for ten years. The first signs of mastery will appear after that time period has passed. Therefore, if someone wants to master themselves, they should spend their first hour each morning on self-improvement and focusing on their mindset and approach to health, spirituality and love.

The entrepreneur and artist now understood how the elite stay ahead. Therefore, they moved on to the next level: cultivating their best selves.

Big Idea #4: Giving attention to each of the four

interior empires will allow you to master yourself and your chosen field.

A billionaire asked, "How often do you hear that there's a secret way to improve your life? There are many people who claim they have the key to helping us change our lives. They say we should think more positively and our lives will be better."

But, said the billionaire, strolling along a white sand beach with his pupils, what these gurus don't tell you is that your Mindset is just one of four "interior empires." If you're only working on your Mindset, you're ignoring your Healthset, your Heartset and Soulset. That's like polishing 25 percent of a picture! Your health set is important because even if you have an amazing mindset it will not work if you're unhealthy physically or mentally. As Sigmund Freud noted "unexpressed emotions will never die." So focus on a healthy heart set to feel better emotionally and physically.

Next, you need to work on your health. Your physical health is important because it helps you live longer and stay productive. What's more, staying fit will help you maintain a high level of energy throughout the day, which in turn will make every day better for you. And that's not all; there's also something else that can make your life even better: cultivating an inner empire.

Billionaires share their wisdom with us. They say that we should remember who we are and what our purpose is. We get pulled into the superficial things in life, so it helps to take time out for ourselves and be alone with our thoughts. In those quiet moments of the early morning, think about what you have to offer the world, then bond with your hero inside of you.

The entrepreneur said that this framework really changed

his perception of himself. The billionaire replied, telling him that he was ready to hear about the 20/20/20 formula, but not in Mauritius, but in Rome. He wanted to be inspired by the passion and architecture of the city and its divine food.

Big Idea #5: The 20/20/20 formula ensures that waking up at 5:00 a.m. generates incredible results.

A billionaire, an entrepreneur and an artist were in Rome. The billionaire said it's time to learn how you can optimize your productivity by moving, reflecting and growing for 20 minutes each day. You could waste your morning on social media or other activities that aren't helpful. But if you use the 20/20/20 formula of getting up early and moving around, reflecting on what matters most to you and growing as a person through meditation or reading something inspirational, then you'll be more productive during the rest of the day.

To feel good, it's important to move your body. You can do this by exercising vigorously for 20 minutes. What's really important is to make yourself sweat because the process of sweating gets rid of cortisol and increases BDNF levels in your brain. This leads to faster thinking and more neural connections between cells in your brain.

Then, you should spend the time between five and six in the morning thinking about what's most important to you. In a world of constant distractions, it will be amazing how much inspiration comes to mind during those few moments of silence before your day starts.

Write these thoughts in a journal. Write down your ambitions, the things you're grateful for in your life, and frustrations that are holding you back. This will help clarify what you want to do with your life and who you really are as a person.

For a few minutes, meditate. There's research that shows it reduces cortisol levels and helps you stay calm. It's the way great performers stay focused on their goals!

Now it's time to grow. Take 20 minutes to learn by reading biographies, learning about human psychology, watching documentaries on innovation or listening to audiobooks about business building. Billionaires have a love of learning in common and you should too.

Here are some ways to start your morning on the right foot and join the 5 AM club.

Big Idea #6: Embracing sleep and the "twin-cycle of elite performance" is essential to maximizing the potential of the 5 AM club.

As Rome slowly came to life, the billionaire entrepreneur and artist went down into the catacombs. The passages were dark and dusty, used by ancient Romans as burial grounds.

The artist asked why they were there and the billionaire explained that it was a good place to discuss the importance of deep sleep.

Studies have shown that sleep is one of the key factors in determining how long you live. It's almost as important to your daily performance as waking up early and getting a good start on your day.

Too many people today are sleep-deprived because of technology. The blue light emitted by our devices reduces melatonin, a chemical that induces sleep. Therefore, it is better to turn off your technology no later than 8:00 p.m., and then spend the rest of the evening talking with loved ones or meditating or relaxing in a bathtub or reading until you go to bed at 10:00 p.m.. That way, you can get enough sleep during your morning hours (5:00 a.m.).

Sleep isn't the only way to refresh yourself. In fact, a key to top performance over time is alternating periods of intense work with periods for relaxation and fun. This process has been discovered by billionaires who have found that it works well for them.

Growth happens not just in the performance phase, but also in the recovery phase. If you want to understand why, said a billionaire, talk to farmers. They'll tell you that there is always an intense period of tilling soil and planting crops after which comes rest or a fallow season when nothing seems to be happening. However, it's during this fallow season that nutrients are replenished and crops really blossom.

Some people don't like to embrace the downtime part of a cycle. The entrepreneur said that if he's not working, he feels guilty. But as the billionaire replied, balance is important. So don't just work; rest and have fun too, knowing it's an essential part of elite performance.

Three biggest lessons learned from this book

Lesson 1: If you want to be successful, give your brain an advantage by waking up at 5 a.m.

The billionaire tells the artist and entrepreneur that he has the key to their success. When they arrive to meet him early the next morning, his first lesson is that waking up at 5 a.m. will give your brain the advantage to succeed throughout the day.

Our minds have a limited amount of "bandwidth." When we fill our day with social media, interactions with those around us, television, and so on, we fill this bandwidth to the point that we can't take in anything more before the day is even over. If you wake up at 5 a.m., you will find you can focus on one thing without these distractions and accomplish much more.

Our brain chemistry is different early in the morning. The brain's prefrontal cortex, or that part of you that makes you worry or analyze things over and over, is temporarily shut down in the peaceful early hours. The tranquility at daybreak also has been shown to increase dopamine and serotonin, helping you feel energized and at peace. What an awesome way to start your day!

Lesson 2: Find balance in all four "interior empires" to find self-mastery.

Here's another valuable lesson about success: don't just focus on mindset. While thinking optimistic thoughts will help you, there are three other "interior empires" when trying to find balance.

Next to your Mindset, you also have your Healthset, Heartset, and Soulset.

Healthset refers to our physical health. One of the best ways to get ahead in life is to live longer. If you want to be in charge of your empire, you need to live long enough to do this! Committing to exercise will help you get much more out of life. It will also help you live longer. It will help you have energy, lose some stress, and be happier.

Heartset is your emotional well-being. To cultivate a healthy emotional life, we need to express ourselves and have healthy emotional attachments. This is vital to our success.

Lastly, Soulset is our spirituality. Whatever you believe, make time in the morning to connect with your spirituality and yourself. Remember all of the things that make you who you are, and why you are doing what you do. Too often we get caught up in the superficiality of life and forget to connect with ourselves deeply.

Apply all these in the peaceful time we make at 5 a.m., and you will be well on your way to a balanced, successful life.

Lesson 3: Use the 20/20/20 formula to set your day up for success.

By now you may be wondering if it's so important to wake up at 5 a.m. What should I do when I'm up so early? It's entirely possible to wake up this early and waste the extra time by using it to watch the news or scroll through social media.

The billionaire, however, lays out the perfect plan: the 20/20/20 rule, which says you should 20 minutes on three highly valuable activities each.

The first 20 minutes of that first hour should consist of exercise. Help your body wake up, and make your body sweat. Sweating decreases cortisol, the hormone responsible for stress and fear. Sweat also releases BDNF, the brain-repairing neurotropic factor, which speeds up the creation of new neural pathways and repairs brain cells. If you want to think quicker, make sure you get sweaty!

The next 20-minute block should consist of reflection and meditation. The peace you find this early will make way for more inspiration than you thought possible. Make time to write these in your journal. Take the time to focus on what you want out of the day before you get distracted. And don't forget meditation, which has been shown to reduce cortisol which will reduce your stress.

Finally, make time to learn. Instead of wasting time on useless entertainment, spend time reading and learning. Learn from the successful people of the world. What all the ultra-rich have in common is a love of learning.

Is the 5 a.m. Club Right For You?

The 5 a.m. club is definitely NOT for you if:

- You currently get up at 8 a.m., 7 a.m., or even 6 a.m. and feel energized, productive, and happy doing it (if it a'int broke, don't fix it)
- You can't consistently get to sleep before 10 p.m. or take a 90-minute nap in the middle of your day.
- You're a night owl and find you're most productive after 6 p.m.
- Your family or social schedule simply don't permit it.
- You aren't able to focus well enough to engage in deep work at 5 a.m.

You don't have to wake up early to be successful...But, to achieve your big goals and dreams you should spend your mornings as productively as possible.

So tomorrow morning, I have a challenge for you.

Instead of waking up one, two, or three hours earlier than you do today. Push back your wake up time by only 15-minutes.

Be the first one out of bed in your house and take advantage of this solitude.

Go downstairs and sit at your kitchen table, armed only with pen and paper. Identify your number one priority in life, whether it's your greatest stress or opportunity and spend these fifteen magical minutes focused on identifying ways to solve the problem or take advantage of the opportunity.

For example, if you are in $5,000 worth of credit card

debt, and that is causing you significant stress, spend the fifteen minutes thinking of ways to cut your expenses and increase your income, and researching how to transfer your debt to a lower interest credit card.

If you do this six days a week, you'll fix your problems, take advantage of the opportunities in your life, and become much more successful — all without cursing the clock each morning or downing 500 mg of caffeine just to function like a normal human.

It's easy to put time on your side, rather than letting it be an enemy in the battle for your day.

A little bit of discipline, in waking up just fifteen minutes earlier, yields great power.

Adding this little bit of structure – rather than going to extremes – brings greater success and freedom into your life without the stress of doing something that's not right for you.

Is the 5am Club Worth Getting out of Bed For?

I came across Robin Sharma's 5am club the way I do most things these days, on Instagram. Ever since reading Sharma's hit book, The Monk Who Sold His Ferrari, I've followed the life coach on social media enjoying the positivity his posts pepper throughout my day. The eight Talisman letters located on the back of the book are passages that hit the nail on the head when it comes to caring about what matters most, and act like a compass for life when you need your priorities realigned. I don't have a guru per se, but if I had to pick one, Sharma would probably be it. So, when he released a book called 'The 5am Club' about a revolutionary morning routine that can change your life for the better, I decided to give the 20/20/20 (movement, reflection and learning) method a shot. I read the book, bought a morning journal, and set a week's worth of 5am alarms on my phone. Armed and (naively thinking I was) ready, here's a take on how it went so you can see if it's right for you.

The Book

Painfully obvious, but trying to join the 5am Club without reading the book and by just reading the below will feel like a baptism of fire. I know because I tried unsuccessfully to 'hack' my induction by reading multiple reviews online. If you're like me and still insist on trying before reading, all you need to do is set your alarm clock for 5am, exercise intensely for the first 20 minutes, meditate/write a journal/plan goals for the second 20 minutes and learn something new for the last 20 minutes.

Early to bed

Setting your alarm at 5am when your usual bedtime

is around 11pm or midnight (like mine) can be painfully hard. It goes completely against everything we've learned about getting eight hours sleep and is unrealistic if you have a baby dictating your evening routine or a job that doesn't allow you to switch off. I averaged about six hours sleep a night during the week but felt the 'sleep for me time' swap was worth it. Using the first 60 minutes of my day for personal preparation made my entire day more productive and intentional, but I had to make significant shifts in my social calendar and evening routine to make it work.

Early to rise

The tag line of 'The 5am Club' is 'own your morning, elevate your life'. It's a big claim, but one that makes sense as it puts you in control of your day and cultivates self-discipline. When my first 5am alarm went off, I pressed snooze so hard I'm surprised my phone didn't break. I mindlessly pulled on my leggings and workout top, grabbed my skipping rope and worked out intensely for 20 minutes per Sharma's advice. I then sat down at my open journal and spent 20 minutes writing morning pages and quarterly goals, before reading a wellness tourism whitepaper for 20 minutes. Because I had prepared everything I needed to move/meditate/learn the night before it made it easy to flow through the routine. The problem was that I was completely exhausted, as I hadn't mastered going to bed early.

Healthy

Sharma's magic morning routine formula can be broken down into three parts, the first of which is working out intensely and sweating for the first 20 minutes. No one ever regrets exercising and the clinically proven benefits of moving more are undisputed, so this is a no brainer. In the words of the productivity master, "Sweating releases BDNG, a brain chemical that actually grows neural connections. Working out also releases dopamine which makes you feel happy." I would skip, go for a short run, do a HIIT workout or a quick Vinyasa flow at home before settling down with a cup of warm water with lemon and some coffee for the next step of the routine.

Wealthy

If time is money and health is wealth, then the 5am Club is definitely worth joining. Not only did I have a lot more time and space to get through my daily to-do list, but I was so much more productive than usual. It also ensured that before my day began, I had time to take care of my priorities and be proactive rather than reactive as the day went on. Waking up so early and dedicating time to workout, meditate, journal, plan, reflect and learn was a game changer and proved to be the biggest takeaway from the experiment. I got through my to-do list faster with zero distractions, didn't feel obliged to look at my phone or email until the workday began, and in general felt a lot more in control. It was good for me physically and mentally, and my business also benefitted.

Wise

The second and third parts of the morning routine include 20 minutes of 'pocketing' (which can include journaling, meditating, visualising, goal setting and planning) and 20 minutes of learning (reading non-fiction, listening to podcasts, learning a language, etc.). My favourite 'pocketing' routine involved 5-10 minutes of morning pages where I write everything that comes to mind down with no structure or plan. I then write down my annual goals and break them down into bi-annual and quarterly steps before pinpointing one important task I can complete that day, which will bring me a step closer to my goal. Setting aside time to do this was quite powerful first thing in the morning. Spending 20 minutes learning something new was also a game changer.

Conclusion

After a week of waking up at the crack of dawn, I decided to adopt the 5am Club morning routine but condensed it and shifted it a little bit to suit my schedule. I don't believe that rigidity suits everyone and I like picking bits and pieces from different methodologies and incorporating them into my life in a way that works for me. I prioritise getting seven or eight hours sleep over waking up at 5am but still set aside 'me time' in the morning to sweat, reflect and learn as I loved the morning routine and found it helped to create some much-needed space in my day and enhanced my productivity and overall wellbeing. I'd recommend giving the 5am Club a shot, but don't be afraid to set your own rules.

Benefits of Waking Up at 5am

Most of us struggle to get out of bed early. I get it, it can be hard to break your routine and get used to waking up at a different time, but I promise you'll thank me for choosing mind over mattress. Some of the most successful people wake up early like Tim Cook, CEO of Apple who starts his day at 3:45am, The Rock is at the gym by 4am every morning, and Richard Branson starts his daily healthy routine at 5:45am. If the greats are a part of the 5am club, why aren't you? Not convinced? Let's break down some of the most important and notable benefits of being early to rise...

- It correlates to better grades or work
- Helps you maintain a healthy diet – late snoozer often skip breakfast, the most important meal of the day!
- It enhances your productivity – there are less distractions early in the morning
- Assists with better mental health by eliminating the stress in the morning (or during the day) of feeling rushed
- Gives you more time to fit in exercise – no more excuses of being too busy
- Improves the quality of your sleep by putting you in more of a consistent routine

Some foods that help in sleeping

Almonds are a type of tree nut with many advantages.

They are an excellent source of many nutrients, as one ounce contains 14% of your daily needs for phosphorus, 32% for manganese and 17% for riboflavin. Also, eating almonds regularly has been associated with lower risks of a few chronic diseases, such as type 2 diabetes and heart disease.

Almonds are also an excellent source of magnesium, providing 19% of your daily needs in only 1 ounce. Consuming adequate amounts of magnesium may help improve sleep quality, especially for those who have insomnia.

Turkey is delicious and nutritious.

It is high in protein, providing 4 grams per ounce (28 grams). Protein is important for keeping your muscles strong and regulating your appetite. Additionally, turkey is a good source of a few vitamins and minerals. A 1-ounce (28-gram) serving contains 5% of your daily needs for riboflavin, 5% for phosphorus and 9% for selenium.

Kiwis are a low-calorie and very nutritious fruit. One medium kiwi contains only 50 calories and a significant amount of nutrients, including 117% of your daily needs for vitamin C and 38% for vitamin K. It also contains a decent amount of folate and potassium, as well as several trace minerals. Furthermore, eating kiwis may benefit your digestive health, reduce inflammation and lower your cholesterol. These effects are due to the high amount of fiber and carotenoid antioxidants that they provide.

Walnuts are a popular type of tree nut.

They are abundant in many nutrients, providing over 19 vitamins and minerals, in addition to 2 grams of fiber, in a 1-ounce (28-gram) serving. Walnuts are particularly rich in magnesium, phosphorus, copper, and manganese.

Additionally, walnuts are a great source of healthy fats, including omega-3 fatty acids and linoleic acid. They also provide 4 grams of protein per ounce, which may be beneficial for reducing appetite.

White rice is a grain that is widely consumed as a staple food in many countries.

The major contrast between white and brown rice is that white rice has had its bran and germ removed, which makes it lower in fiber, nutrients, and antioxidants. Nevertheless, white rice still contains a decent amount of a few vitamins and minerals. A 3.5-ounce (100-gram) serving of white rice provides 14% of your daily needs for folate, 11% for thiamin and 24% for manganese.

Workout and Sleep

Workout can give a boost to your sleeping habits in various ways these include:

- Improve Sleep Quality
- Productive Sleep
- Reduce Stress, insomnia, and anxiety.

More than a third of American adults are not getting enough sleep on a regular basis, according to a new study in the Centers for Disease Control and Prevention's (CDC) Morbidity and Mortality Weekly Report. This is the first study to document estimates of self-reported healthy sleep duration (7 or more hours per day) for all 50 states and the District of Columbia.

The American Academy of Sleep Medicine and the Sleep Research Society recommend that adults aged 18–60 years sleep at least 7 hours each night to promote optimal health and well-being.

Sleeping less than seven hours per day is associated with an increased risk of developing chronic conditions such as obesity, diabetes, high blood pressure, heart disease, stroke, and frequent mental distress.

Book Review: The 5AM Club

The 5AM Club has clawed its way into my mind and refuses to leave.

Robin Sharma's The 5AM Club is essentially self-help fan-fiction. The novel starts with a female entrepreneur attending a self-help conference where a famous "Spellbinder" collapses partway through his session and almost everyone leaves. The entrepreneur and her seat buddy are accosted by a homeless man who turns out to be a billionaire. He offers to teach them what the Spellbinder taught him — free of charge on his beautiful private island, and it's all paid for. This is about five chapters in, and I had to google if the story was real or not — it's not.

Since chapter five, the billionaire hints about the 20/20/20 rule, which dictates the way we should spend the precious hour between five and six am. It isn't until chapter 13 that the reader finds out what it is. The rule is simple — spend 20 minutes doing some physical activities, 20 minutes doing something introspective (like meditating or journaling) and the last 20 minutes should be spent growing as a person (which could be reading a book, watching an educational video or listening to an educational podcast). This is actually a good idea of how to spend an hour.

Chapter 15 and 16 are a summary of everything in the book — basically what I was expecting the entire book to be. If the author had written all of the steps and ideas without a frame story, it would probably be closer to the size of a pamphlet instead of a book.

I don't think there is anything too special about this book compared to other self-help books. It's all the same general knowledge like have a morning routine, and getting up at 5 a.m. gives you extra time for yourself. As someone who gets up at 5:30 a.m. everyday, I nod to certain parts of the story. Most people aren't up, so you don't need to check your emails or get back to people yet. The book does have good points, even if they're little cheesy like "we are all special" and "there never has nor ever will be someone like you with your experiences and gifts."

Overall, the book was filled with a pointless, infuriating and unrealistic story. I found myself wondering why the author did not interview anyone who is successful because they wake up at 5 a.m. Instead, Robin Sharma wrote a lavish production whose kernels of wisdom are boiled down in two chapters at the end. I enjoy reading fiction and I enjoy self-help books, but the 5am Club is the worst combination of both.

Printed in Great Britain
by Amazon